AF574028

Burrowing Birds

by Anita Gustafson
Illustrated by Joel Schick

Lothrop, Lee & Shepard Books
New York

 Inquiries should be addressed to Lothrop, Lee & Shepard Books, a division of William Morrow & Company, Inc., 105 Madison Avenue, New York, New York 10016. Printed in the United States of America.
First Edition. 1 2 3 4 5 6 7 8 9 10

Library of Congress Cataloging in Publication Data
Gustafson, Anita.
Burrowing birds.
Includes index.
SUMMARY: Discusses varieties of birds that burrow underground to nest, including the kookaburra, shearwater, kiwi, burrowing owl, common shelduck, crab plover, and the blue-crowned motmot. 1. Birds—Juvenile literature. 2. Burrowing animals—Juvenile literature. [1. Birds. 2. Burrowing animals]
I. Schick, Joel. II. Title.
QL676.2.G87 598.2′564 80-29058
ISBN 0-688-41977-1 ISBN 0-688-51977-6 (lib. bdg.)

Contents

List of Illustrations

Burrowing Owl

1

Walking Over Birds

When naturalist Ronald Lockley wanted to study migration, he went out one night to catch a bird. He didn't bother taking a net. To catch his bird, Lockley took a shovel.

As the sun set, he landed his boat on an island off Wales. He got out, took his shovel, and walked around. When he found a likely-looking spot, he dug carefully.

A few minutes later, he had a strong, healthy bird. So he could identify the bird later, he banded its leg. Then he put the bird in a crate and the crate in his boat.

In a short while, the banded bird was flying over the Atlantic Ocean to Boston—in a plane. And only fourteen days later, that same bird had flown back to its home on the island—with its own wings!

The bird was a Manx Shearwater. From the moment Lockley stepped ashore, he had been walking over these birds. He heard them calling in the twilight, but he didn't see one until after he had dug it up. All the shearwaters on the island were hidden underground.

Far away in the Pacific Ocean are other islands. One of them is off Australia.

If you came to this island, you wouldn't find trees. In fact, you wouldn't find much of anything, except some tall grass growing in the sand. All day long, the island is quiet. Maybe a breeze ruffles the grass, but the grass is all that moves. The island seems deserted and useless.

But just wait until the sun sets!

As the darkness grows, a bird appears out at sea. It flies swiftly and silently to the island. It lands and is suddenly gone. It disappears! Now more and more birds appear from the sea, as if by magic. Soon the air is filled with their wheeling, whirling flight.

Birds flash up around you, darting in from all sides. There are thousands of birds, and thousands more behind them. The flight of the birds is eerie—a riot of quiet wings. It goes on and on and on, for half an hour or more.

Thousands of birds that don't call and don't cry drain from the sea. Only their wings jar the air as they come to land—and disappear.

Little by little the flight falls apart. The incoming birds thin out. The last ones straggle in and come to land. These are swallowed out of sight.

And there is silence for a moment.

Then noise erupts. Noise fills the night. Gurgles! Groans! Chortles! Hoarse laughter! But there isn't a bird in sight.

The noises come from five feet down. They come from the nests of the Short-tailed Shearwaters.

All day long this island only *seemed* to be deserted. The

baby shearwaters were there all the time, down in their underground nests. All day long as you walked on this island, you were walking over birds.

It's no wonder you didn't hear them. The fat, downy babies were quiet. Each one waited in its own private nest. It plucked grass from the walls with its black bill. It tucked the grass around itself. The baby shearwaters spent the day quietly making their own soft beds.

Now the grown-ups are home. The little shearwaters, or "mutton-birds," are being fed and catching up on family news.

Actually, you don't have to go to far-flung islands to walk over birds. All over the world are birds that shun the treetops, that don't care for a nest on the ground. From mountaintop to riverbank to level prairie land are birds that choose to nest only where they're hidden underground.

2
The Underground Birds

Who are the underground birds?

Some of them are "squatters." They take over another animal's burrow.

If rabbits leave their burrow in a sand dune, a pair of Shelduck may move in. Sweeping marks on the sand at ebb tide say a Shelduck is around. The bird finds its food by sweeping its bill back and forth in an arc in shallow water, leaving marks in the sand. Not far away, in the burrow, the female Shelduck may shelter up to sixteen white eggs.

A few birds that have found "squatting" convenient stay with certain digging animals. Pika are small burrowing rodents that live in mountains. They dig their burrows close together, making Pika towns. Around every Pika town in the high mountains of Tibet are Snow Finches. These Tibetan finches move into any vacant burrows.

Sometimes "squatters" are a part of a large underground community. The Burrowing Owl is one of these birds. In dry grasslands, like the southwestern plains of the United States,

ommon Shelduck

Snow Finch

there are few large trees and many predators. So the Burrowing Owl joins snakes and ferrets and prairie dogs underground where there is safety from the large animals that walk the surface.

Burrowing Owls can dig their own burrows if they want to. Unlike most other burrowing birds, these owls use only their feet to dig. But usually they don't bother. They move into a burrow abandoned by another member of their underground community. Sometimes their new home is too small. Then the Burrowing Owls will make it larger by scraping away the earth and kicking it outside into a mound.

But the most intriguing underground birds are the ones that do all their own digging—the burrowing birds.

Some don't dig very deeply. In New Zealand, the parrot Kakapo and the pear-shaped Kiwi search around tree roots. When they find a hole already there, they dig it out a little more.

Both these birds live their entire lives on the ground. They can't fly. The Kiwi's wings don't work at all. The Kakapo's wings merely help it flutter *down* from a rock or tree it has *climbed*. Hiding in a burrow helps protect the birds from enemies such as dogs and cats.

A bird doesn't have to be flightless to be a burrowing bird, however. Surprisingly, many birds that are expert fliers are also expert diggers. Some of the best aviators in the bird world can burrow as far as fifteen feet into the earth!

A few birds are expert excavating engineers. On Whero Island off New Zealand, five different kinds of petrels and shearwaters burrow. Each kind digs its nest into a different

Kakapo

layer of the soil. Whero Island is a real underground city! Instead of high-rise apartments, the island has deep-down burrows.

There are underground birds with familiar names. Some starlings, woodpeckers, and pigeons burrow. Kingfishers and their relatives dig down to nest. Most gulls and terns lay their eggs in scrapes in sand or on the bare shore, but the Inca Tern *(Larosterna inca)* may use niches, hollows, rock caverns, or underground burrows it has enlarged itself.

There are burrowing birds that perch and sing. Perching birds, or passerines, are the most numerous group of birds, and most passerines are songbirds. The Sand Martins of England and Europe are the same species as our Bank Swallow. They are songbirds, and they nest underground. In England, all the Sand Martins in a community help dig each other's burrows. When all the burrows are finished, each pair of Sand Martins pays attention to only what's happening in its own burrow.

There are burrowing birds that like to wade. The Crab Plover, a wading bird from Africa, burrows into sandbanks. Young Crab Plovers are born with a coat of down. They can run right after they hatch. But their parents still bring crabs and other crunchy things to feed them in their burrows.

There are burrowing birds that love the sea. Puffins burrow into cliffs and under grass sod in the north. One kind of penguin burrows in the south. Prions and storm-petrels and shearwaters live most of their lives at sea. All these sea-loving birds come to land for only one reason—to go into a burrow and nest.

Sand Martin

Crab Plover

All these and more are burrowing birds. They use their bills as pickaxes and their feet as shovels. They dig a tunnel that ends in a room, a larger nesting chamber. They were born knowing how to do this.

A burrow nest is a secret place. It's meant to hide what's inside. And the burrowing birds like it that way. A dark underground nest is the only place they will raise a family.

3

A Kingfisher Family Underground

The European Kingfisher sits on a willow branch above the river. The bird is small, only six inches long. Sun glints off his metallic blue-green back.

He doesn't move. His keen eyes watch the water carefully for signs of food. He and his mate have staked out an exclusive claim to this territory. No other kingfisher is welcome to fish in these waters!

This is the second year the kingfisher couple has come here. Last year, they dug a burrow.

Together, they found a sandy bank. They struck the sand with their strong, dagger-shaped bills to make a hole. They worked hard. Soon they had dug a hole two and one-half inches across. They went on digging. The tunnel grew longer. Their feet shoveled out the loose soil. Finally, they had dug three feet into the bank.

Now they hollowed out a nest chamber. They raised their first family there. When the little ones were ready, they left the burrow. Their parents left with them. The family split up, but the burrow remained.

Common Kingfisher

The kingfisher pair have come back to that burrow this year. The female is in the nest chamber now. She is sitting on three precious eggs, incubating them by keeping them warm. She will lay eggs for several more days, probably one every other day.

Suddenly the kingfisher sees something move in the water. He doesn't move immediately. He waits until his sharp eyes tell him that the movement is a small fish.

Food!

The kingfisher dives from his perch like lightning and plunges into the water. He seizes the fish with his bill. The fish wiggles, tries to escape. The kingfisher rises to the surface, the fish still flopping. The bird takes his prey to a nearby perch, kills it, and swallows it headfirst.

He has eaten, but he hasn't finished fishing. His next catch will be for his mate. She needs a lot to eat while she is laying eggs.

He turns again to his study of the water. He sees a fish and dives to catch it. This time, he flies home with it at once.

The floor of the nest chamber is littered. Heads and wings from last year's dragonflies lie around. Bones and scales from fish clutter the chamber. Kingfishers eat a fish or insect whole, then cast up what they can't digest.

The resulting litter is the only cushion the eggs have. Without it, there would be no nest lining at all. The litter is soft, much like a pile of cigar ash.

The kingfisher offers a fish to his mate. He holds it so she can swallow it headfirst. Then he leaves the burrow and returns to the river. Along the way, he sees another movement in the water. He hovers in mid-air for a moment. No, it isn't something to eat, so he doesn't dive. He flies on to his willow branch.

Time goes on in this peaceful way, until five to eight white eggs lie in the dark nest. The kingfisher nest we're watching now holds eight eggs.

Three weeks later, the young kingfishers hatch. The babies are helpless, born blind and naked. The only movement they can make is to lift their heads and open their bills. This is called *gaping*. Gaping is the way baby birds cry for food. Both parents must work to feed the hungry young.

Within a few days the babies' eyes open, and they can see the light that comes from the tunnel entrance. The mother kingfisher enters the burrow with food. As she does, the burrow grows darker for a moment. The shadow makes the babies gape.

The one nearest the entrance opens wide. Its mother puts her bill deep into the open mouth. She brings up food from her own throat to feed the baby bird. When the baby is finished, it moves away quietly.

Meanwhile, its seven brothers and sisters have formed a circle. As each baby is fed, the others move up a place. One by one each of the young ones get a share. Mealtime in a kingfisher burrow is an orderly affair when the food supply is ample.

The babies stay inside the burrow. For three or four weeks, their parents come often to feed them.

Since the burrow was dug on a slant, most of the waste flows out. Still, the nest is not a pleasant place. Between feeding visits the parents bathe often, splashing and diving in their river.

But the babies manage quite well. Soon they are fledged: they have their feathers. They are ready to fly out into the world. When they do, the family breaks up.

The burrow is empty and quiet. But it will be there for another family, another year. The kingfisher couple will wait until the spring floods are over. When the water runs clear, it will be easy for them to fish. Then they'll reclaim their territory. They'll come back to their burrow. Another cycle of kingfisher family life will begin.

Ancient peoples admired the kingfisher's beauty. They told many stories and legends about the bird.

More than two thousand years ago, people didn't know that kingfishers were burrowing birds. They thought kingfishers laid and incubated their eggs on the surface of the ocean. When this happened, they said, the weather was calm and beautiful.

We know now that kingfishers raise their families underground, but we still admire the bird's bright beauty just as people did long ago. And the kingfisher family life is a good story in itself.

4

Excavating Kingfisher Cousins

The European Kingfisher has many close relatives. We'll call them cousins. The most familiar cousin lives in Australia. A famous song tells how this merry old king(fisher) sits in an old gum tree and laughs. You've probably already guessed the name of this cousin.

If you said *Kookaburra,* you were right.

The Kookaburra is also known as the "laughing jackass." That name comes from the way it calls at dawn or just after sunset.

This is one of the largest of the kingfisher cousins. It's seventeen inches long—about three times as big as the European Kingfisher. There are other differences between the two cousins. The Kookaburra isn't as brightly colored and it doesn't fish for food. It likes snails and lizards and slugs and snakes. It's also happy munching crabs and insects. In fact, a Kookaburra will eat almost anything. It even roams around towns, scavenging what people throw out.

A Kookaburra does like to raise its family in the dark as

Kookaburra

Blue-crowned Motmot

its cousin does—but with a twist. It doesn't burrow into the ground. Instead, it burrows into a termite nest!

In Australia, termite nests can be gigantic. Those on the ground can tower as high as twenty-three feet! The nests begin below the surface, so they're even bigger than they look. The whole nest has a tough outer layer like a thick skin.

At least fifty kinds of birds, including Kookaburras, like to nest with termites. They peck on the nest's tough skin to make a hole. The termites at first try to fight off the intruders. Then they seem to accept matters. They carefully build up a partition between the bird's nest and their own. They'll live in what's left of their nest.

Kookaburras finish their "nest within a nest" and lay two or three white eggs in it. After the young have grown up and flown away, the termites repair the hole and go on as before.

Other kingfisher cousins prefer to burrow into the ground. One prepares the burrow ahead of the time its family will need it. This cousin is the Blue-crowned Motmot.

Motmots live in forest clearings in Central and South America. Usually they live alone. But one day, one Motmot sees another through the leaves.

The two Motmots look good to each other, with their green backs and blue heads and tails decorated with "racquets." When the birds preen, they use their beaks to smooth and clean their feathers. During the preening process some of the loosely attached vanes on their tail feathers are pulled off. The remaining vanes look like racquets at the ends of their foot-long tails.

As they study each other, the Motmots swing their tails from side to side like a pendulum in a clock. Soon a pair bond—a bird marriage—is made. Now, even though they are usually solitary, the two work as a team.

It is the rainy season. The ground is soft. The two Motmots dig a long tunnel in a soft bank. The burrow can be as long as fifteen feet. But when it's finished, the Motmots leave!

They have prepared the tunnel in advance of the coming dry season, when the ground will be too hard for them to dig. When the dry season comes, the Motmots return to their waiting burrow. Without bothering to decorate or line their nest in any way, the female lays her three to four white eggs on the bare floor.

Now the two Motmots are even more a team. They both incubate the eggs until they hatch. Both feed and care for the young, which are blind and naked at birth. Together they bring insects, small lizards, and fruit to their young. Little Motmots—and their parents—especially like bananas.

Motmots aren't fishing birds. But they catch insects with the same swift, sure flight the European Kingfisher uses in fishing. Motmots sit on a branch, tails ticking back and forth. Then, suddenly, they dart from their perch. Sometimes they pluck insects right from the air. Sometimes they seize a hard-shelled beetle from the forest floor. Little teeth on their bills hold the beetle firmly. The birds return to their perch and eat.

Todies are another kingfisher cousin. They are smaller than the other cousins—only three and one half to five inches long. The plump little birds are green on top, white or yellow on the stomach, and they all wear a bright red bib.

Jamaican Tody

Todies are found only on islands in the West Indies. One kind lives on Jamaica, another on Puerto Rico, another on Cuba, and two more on Hispaniola. Their choice of neighborhood, or habitat, all depends on which island they're from. Some Todies live in tropical forests and others in grasslands.

All Todies share a liking for underground nests. A pair digs a burrow which is up to twenty-five inches long. They share incubation of the two to four eggs. Both tend and feed the young when they hatch.

They hunt insects for their little ones, their feathers making a rattling sound as they fly. Todies aren't as free and easy in the air as the other kingfishers. But they're quick enough to find lots to eat. Their bills have teeth, too, just as the Motmots' do.

Kingfisher cousins, like the European Kingfisher, pair off. The male and female of each couple raise their family together. In fact, it has been said that ninety percent of all birds follow this pattern.

But a few birds have more help around the nest. One kind that does is also an excavating kingfisher cousin.

5

Underground Aunts and Uncles and Others

Who is the kingfisher cousin that has its own "aunts and uncles" to help underground?

The bright-colored, friendly, fast-flitting Bee-eater.

Baby Red-throated Bee-eaters are born into a big, close-knit family. Their parents are mated for life. But even without their parents, the young ones wouldn't be alone in the world. In the underground nests of the Bee-eaters are helpers —sometimes as many as five other birds—that tirelessly help the parents raise the little ones.

The helpers are single. Most are young adults that aren't ready to have their own families, so they help the older pair. Most of the helpers are males—"uncles." About one-third are "aunts." Often they were born in the same area.

Uncles and aunts get into the family act early. They help the older couple dig a nest in a bank. All Bee-eaters are agile and completely at home in the air. And they need to be to begin a burrow!

In the air they back away from the bank, sometimes several

Red-throated Bee-eater

yards, sometimes only inches. They open their beaks a little and hurl themselves through the air at the bank. Each time, they chip away some of the soil.

As soon as the hole is large enough, they get a foothold. They go on digging with their beaks. Bee-eaters dig faster and faster the farther in they go.

Chip! Chip! Three feet in. They kick the loose soil out with their feet. Chip! Kick! Chip! Kick! Seven feet in. Chip-chip! Kickkick! Sometimes they tunnel ten feet in. When they're finished with the tunnel, they hollow out a nest chamber.

Now the parent birds take over. When two to five white eggs lie on the bare floor of the chamber, the aunts and uncles help incubate them. When the young ones hatch, aunts and uncles help feed them, too. They bring bees and wasps.

Sound good? Not to us, but Bee-eaters are specialists at preparing their food.

The Red-throated Bee-eater swoops on flying bees from a perch and then carries the bee back to the perch. It rubs and pounds the bee or wasp on the branch to kill or stun it before eating it, and in the process the bee discharges its venom. Now the bee is ready to eat and the Bee-eater eats it.

With so many grown-ups helping, baby Bee-eaters get a lot to eat. The hard heads of the bees are cast up and left in the nest. As many as 2,753 bee's heads have been counted in a single Bee-eater nest!

Puffbirds also have help with their little ones. These birds are woodpecker cousins. Puffbirds have big heads and short necks. They look squat and puffy. When they're comfortable and safe, they raise their feathers until they look like big, soft powderpuffs.

One of the larger puffbirds is the White-fronted Nunbird. It lives in tropical forests. A parent pair excavates a tunnel into level ground. They hide the entrance with dead leaves and twigs, and they carpet the nest chamber with more dead leaves. Working together, they incubate three glossy white eggs.

So far, the Nunbird sounds as usual as any other burrowing bird. But when the babies hatch, unusual things begin to happen. Father Nunbird stays at home with the babies. And mother goes out to bring home the bacon—insects, in this case.

She catches and prepares her food the same way Bee-eaters catch and prepare theirs. She has a lot of help from three to five other birds. But these helpers aren't aunts and uncles. They are the family she and her mate raised the year before—big brothers and sisters!

All these grown-ups bring food to the newborns, but they don't make it easy. The adults bring food to the entrance of the tunnel and call. Then they wait.

The baby Nunbirds are blind when they are newly born. Inside the nest, they can barely move. But they are hungry, so the little Nunbirds grope inch by inch along five feet of tunnel. Somehow they make the trip and take their food from the grown-up's bill.

Four weeks later, the young ones are ready to leave. They fly out of the nest and immediately head for the top of the forest canopy. The grown-ups continue to bring food for them, but they still don't make it easy.

Vhite-fronted Nunbird

Now they perch a short distance from the young birds to call. The young must dart from their perch and snatch the food on the wing. It sounds mean, but it isn't. The little birds are learning what they will need to know later. They are being trained to hunt and catch their own food.

6

Weird Underground Guests

Usually a nest is home for only one family of birds. The family includes parents and their young. But we've seen that sometimes the family includes aunts and uncles, and sometimes big sisters and brothers. And sometimes a bird's "family" includes other, more surprising guests.

Fairy Prions welcome weird guests to their burrows on islands off New Zealand. Their guests are Tuataras—prehistoric monsters!

The Tuatara looks like a lizard, but it isn't. It's so unusual that it has been classified all by itself. It has no living relatives.

An unbroken line of Tuataras stretches back 200 million years. In all that time, the animal hasn't changed. It is a living fossil. Today's Tuataras look just the same as their ancestors did. They still have a white, papery crest running along their backs. They still have spiked tails. They still have three eyes, too.

The third eye sits on top of the head between the two real eyes. You can see the eye in young Tuataras. In older

Fairy Prion

Tuataras, scales cover the third eye. No one is quite sure what the purpose of the third eye is. Or was.

Prions and Tuataras have a living arrangement. During the day, the Prions are off eating at sea. When they're full and the sun is setting, the little Prions flit home. Like swallows, they fly delicately and expertly. Once on land, however, Prions are clumsy. As they shuffle to their burrows, they may meet their much larger guests coming out. The Tuataras have made themselves at home in the Prions' burrows all day. At night, they go out to catch beetles and crickets to eat.

This day-shift/night-shift arrangement works well for the adult Prions and the Tuataras. But baby Prions stay in the burrow day *and* night, and no one has discovered how *they* feel about it. What do you suppose a baby Prion thinks each morning when a Tuatara slouches in? Would you leave your little sister with a three-eyed monster all day long? Prions would and do—and it all seems to work out!

7

Penguins and Puffins

Every evening toward sundown, tourists gather near Melbourne, Australia. They come to watch the nightly march of the Little Penguins. It is not a stately march. It is not a dignified parade. The penguins are natural, lovable comedians.

And they are little—the smallest penguins in the world. Each one weighs only one and one-half pounds when it's full-grown. It stands sixteen inches tall. Its stomach is white and the rest is bluish gray. Because of its size and color, a Little Penguin is often called "Fairy Penguin" or "Little Blue Penguin."

They *march* from the sea because they can't fly. They are comical because they just aren't made to be graceful or dignified on land. Their legs are set far back on their bodies. This makes them stand stiffly upright. Let's face facts—the Little Penguins don't really march, either. They hop.

On they come, hopping from rock to rock, teetering each time they land. They pause every now and then, throw back

Little Penguin

their heads, and bray like happy little donkeys. Then on they hop from place to place, tottering with every hop.

Braying is the way the penguins talk to each other. Sailors hear them bray at sea, too, where these birds are more comfortable. The wings that can't fly through air are perfect for flying through water. The feet that are clumsy on land steer skillfully in the sea. Penguins are graceful swimmers and strong divers.

Then why do they ever leave the water?

All penguins come in from the sea to raise their families. Two species migrate to gather in huge colonies in Antarctica. One species lays a single egg on the ice. The other lays two eggs in sand or a scrape in the bare ground. But a few penguins are burrowing birds. The Little Penguin is one of these. It stays around Australia and New Zealand and it raises its young underground.

Each couple digs its own burrow. After two eggs are laid, one parent stays home to incubate them. The other goes off to eat in the sea. The one at home doesn't get anything to eat until the two parents switch duties. When that happens, the hungry parent goes to sea and the other one incubates.

They continue to switch duties after the babies hatch. The stay-at-home partner remains in the burrow most of the time, but sometimes it gets out for a breather at night. The returning parent feeds the young ones with a milky liquid from its throat.

The babies are covered with a glossy light-gray coat of fine down at first. A couple of weeks later, a duller, brown coat appears. The baby penguins grow more and more active, but still they remain in the burrow. In about six weeks the coarse brown down has disappeared and feathers have grown. Now the young ones leave the nest. They start swimming in the sea. They discover that they can feed themselves. They don't return to the burrow.

Now their parents go out to sea to eat and gain weight. They *do* return to the burrow. It is time for their annual molt. When they molt, they lose their old feathers and grow new ones.

Their molt takes about two weeks. During that time, the adult Little Penguins won't eat anything. They stay in the burrow, looking ragged and sad. They smooth their growing feathers constantly with their bills. When the new feathers are all sleekly in place the adult Little Penguins will leave the burrow, too.

Their burrow has protected their family as it grew. But it has done more than that. It protected them, too, while they were without feathers and unable to catch food.

Penguins live south of the equator. At the opposite end of the world, far in the north, live the puffins. Penguins and puffins are not cousins. They aren't related at all, but they look as if they *should* be.

Puffins are clownish, too. Their legs are set well back on the body as a penguin's legs are. So puffins, too, stand upright. And, like penguins, puffins are expert swimmers and strong divers. They use their wings to fly underwater.

And puffins can also fly through air. They need to get up speed before they can take off. So they run down a slope and launch themselves from a cliff into the air. They stay aloft

Puffin

by pumping their wings furiously. They can also take off from the waves.

The Common Puffin dresses up like a clown when it is time to raise a family. Bright red, yellow, and black plates grow on its large bill. Three small horny plates grow around its eyes. Its feet become bright red.

The pairs of Common Puffins look gay and festive as they look for soft ground. They'll dig a burrow up to four feet long and line the nesting chamber with a thin layer of grass.

The single white egg hatches in about six weeks. For the next six weeks, until it's fully grown, the little puffin stays in its burrow. Its parents will bring it fish to eat.

Puffins catch fish by chasing them underwater. When they catch one, they hold it crosswise between their tongue and upper jaw. By storing fish in this way, they can still open their beaks to catch more.

A puffin parent returns with a beakful of fish—up to thirty at one time! It enters the burrow laughing. Close your mouth and laugh deep in your throat and you'll hear the sound a parent puffin makes. Does it sound as if you've got a surprise?

"Ha-ha-ha," the parent puffin seems to laugh. "Look what I've got for you!"

Parent puffins return with food for their little one for about six weeks. The baby grows fat. Then, one day, the parent puffins don't come back. By this time they have lost their gay clown clothes. The plates on their bills and around their eyes have fallen off. Their feet have turned gray. Once again they are a sober gray and black and white, and will remain so until time for their next family.

When that time comes around again, many puffins will gather together in their breeding grounds. Puffins are highly colonial birds. Their nesting areas are often so filled with burrows that the surface of the ground looks like a honeycomb.

But for this year, the parent puffins have finished their family duties. The abandoned chick stays alone in its burrow, living on its fat and growing its flight feathers. After a week, the hungry chick leaves the burrow one night and flutters out to sea by itself.

Perhaps this sounds sad to us. It isn't. By the time the parent puffins leave their little one, it is ready to be on its own.

And Common Puffins care about each other. If one is hurt, others come to it. They swim around the injured bird and push it with their bills. They try to help however they can.

Puffins and penguins may *look* funny sometimes, but they really aren't silly at all!

8

Wave-walkers and Shearwaters

The soot-brown, seven-inch birds walk on the water behind a fishing boat. One of them holds its feet together. It bounds from wave to wave, looking as if it is on springs. Another patters over the water, lowering one yellow, webbed foot at a time. All of the birds spread their long wings. They keep them spread and motionless.

The fishermen like to see them. They say it's unlucky to hurt one of these "Mother Carey's chickens."

The birds are Wilson's Storm-Petrels. And they really aren't walking at all. The wind holds them up by the wings. They are drifting with the wind. They are so light that it is hard for them to slow down enough to feed. They dip their feet to act as brakes.

They eat tiny water animals floating on the surface of the waves. The fishermen toss oily fish livers onto the water. The birds especially like these.

Sailors believe they can forecast weather by the way the storm-petrels behave. If the birds sit quietly on the water, the sailors say, that means calm weather.

Wilson's Storm-Petrel

But storm-petrels seldom sit and rest on the water. They fly over the water almost all the time. And the only time they rest on land is when they go underground to nest.

The "wave-walking" storm-petrels and their close relatives, the shearwaters, are tireless travelers. They keep to an exact schedule. You can almost tell what month it is by the arrival and departure of these birds.

The calendar of the Wilson's Storm-Petrel looks like this:

NOVEMBER

Gather at breeding grounds in the Antarctic.

(Seasons in the southern half of the world are the opposite of those in the Northern Hemisphere. November is the beginning of the Southern Hemisphere's summer. The sea ice breaks up now. Food can be gathered from the waters. The storm-petrels will need it to feed to their young. Pairs of birds rejoin each other by their old burrows. The tunnel leads through hard black ice and grit to the nesting chamber.)

DECEMBER

Lay one egg.

(Sometimes the nest chamber is not lined. Other times there is a thick lining of Adelie Penguin feathers. Often there is clutter from previous years.)

Incubate egg.

(Storm-petrels share this duty with each other. After thirty-five days, the baby birds hatch. They are blind and naked when they are first born, but they soon open their eyes and begin to grow feathers.)

JANUARY

Feed baby.

FEBRUARY

Keep feeding baby.

MARCH

Feed baby some more.

(By the time late March rolls around, the baby weighs twice as much as either of its parents! It is fat and it will need its fat.)

APRIL

Leave baby.

(The Southern Hemisphere's winter is setting in. The adults desert the young to fly north into the Northern

Hemisphere's summer. For a while the baby uses its fat to grow flying feathers and muscles. It gets hungry. It leaves the burrow and follows the route taken by its parents. The young bird learns to feed itself as it flies.)

MAY

Fly.

(The storm-petrels move along the Atlantic coasts of North and South America.)

JUNE

Fly.

(By June, the storm-petrels are spread out all over the North Atlantic. None are found in the Southern Hemisphere now.)

JULY, AUGUST

Fly.

(The storm-petrels fly and feed all over the North Atlantic.)

SEPTEMBER

Fly.

(The storm-petrels gather along the west coast of Africa.)

OCTOBER

Fly.

(They loop back across the Atlantic Ocean to the coast of South America.)

NOVEMBER

Fly to gather at breeding grounds in the Antarctic.

The calendar of the Wilson's Storm-Petrels is repeated year after year. They make an annual tour of the Atlantic Ocean. One of the several kinds of shearwaters called "mutton birds" —the Short-tailed Shearwater—makes an even longer trip. They fly 20,000 miles every year! Their flight pattern is a figure eight over the Pacific Ocean.

This shearwater's journey is regular and exact, too. At the end of September, Short-tailed Shearwaters arrive on their breeding islands near Australia. They repair their burrows and fly back out to sea. They return about November 20. Each of the millions of female shearwaters lays her single egg within the next twenty days. In fact, most of the eggs are laid between November 24 and 26. The shearwater calendar is very regular!

Right on schedule, the shearwaters leave their nesting grounds in April and May. Flights of shearwaters can number 150 million individuals. And they all follow their Pacific flight pattern. They return to nest on schedule about November 20, repeating their calendar.

Shearwater

Both storm-petrel and shearwater babies are left in the burrow alone for long periods of time after they hatch. And both are bigger than their parents by the time the parents stop feeding them. Their parents have found a way to bring back a lot of food at each feeding.

They pre-digest. A fish is mostly (70%) water. Pre-digestion presses out the water—and the weight of the water. These birds fly long distances to get enough to eat for themselves and their young one. If they had to carry around water, it would take too much of their energy. But because they can concentrate the food, the birds can carry back enough thick fish soup to last its young one until the next feeding in three or four or five days.

9

The Strange Case of the Rare River Martins

A nest underground is meant to hide what happens inside, and it does this very well. One bird goes a step further. Even its burrowing grounds are hidden most of the year.

Africa is dry in February and March. The Congo River runs low. So does the nearby Ubangi. Sandbanks grow in the middle of these rivers as the water level falls.

Then flocks of black birds appear. They have red beaks and red eyes. The 5½-inch-long birds fly effortlessly and beautifully. They circle and soar over the sandbanks, and finally settle on them.

The birds are African River Martins. They have come to the sandbanks, the temporary islands, to nest.

They dig their burrows down into the sand. The tunnel ends in a chamber which they line with dead leaves and twigs. They lay three white eggs.

The eggs hatch and the young grow, eating the winged ants and other insects brought to them. The adults feed as they fly, never alighting on the land.

Soon the young birds are ready to fly. And just in time!

The rains begin to fall. The rivers rise. The sandbanks are flooded, the burrows submerged.

Now the flocks of black birds again rise in the sky. They wheel and circle. Water laps over their nesting ground, hiding all traces of the birds' nests. The River Martins migrate down the rivers for five hundred miles to find shelter on the African coast.

Once there were many River Martins in a large, widespread family. Slowly the family disappeared. Ornithologists —scientists who study birds—thought that the African River Martin was the only family member left on earth.

There was mystery about the bird's habits. Where and how did it nest? That question was answered only sixty years ago. The breeding grounds were discovered before the floodwaters hid them.

In 1968, another discovery was made. Ornithologists in Thailand were netting birds to learn more about their migration patterns. They found an unknown bird in their nets.

The small, swallow-like bird was black. It had a green bill, white rump and eyes, and a special structure in its tail that showed it was another River Martin. The White-eyed River Martin is the only other known survivor of this once-great family. The two small birds are cousins separated by 6,000 miles!

The case of the rare River Martins is strange.

It is even more strange that the African River Martin is a burrowing bird. It is a flying artist. It would happily fly through the whole of its life, and it could do it. Yet it doesn't nest in the high, waving treetops. Why would it rather nest underground?

10

Why Does a Bird Go Underground?

It is strange that a bird as free in the air as the African River Martin is would burrow underground to nest. Why does *any* bird go underground?

The first birds probably simply laid their eggs on the ground. Some birds continue to nest in this way today. But other birds began nesting in natural holes—pockets in the ground or places between rocks. The next step was to burrow out those natural hiding places a little more. Some birds found this to their advantage and they went on burrowing, going farther and farther into the ground.

While other birds took to chipping out holes in trees or to building all the many other kinds of nests, the burrowing birds stuck with their own kind of nest. It fit them precisely. Their burrows helped them survive. The almost flightless Kakapo and the molting Little Penguin still today find protection from enemies in their burrows.

But probably even more important to burrowing birds is the protection the burrows give their families. A nest underground helps the young from the time they are encased in an eggshell to the time they wear flying feathers.

A snug burrow helps parent birds incubate their eggs. The earth acts as insulation, keeping the temperature steady inside.

Take a look at what happens high in the Andes Mountains in South America. Here many birds burrow—doves, ducks, woodpeckers, ovenbirds, to name a few. Outside, the temperature shoots up and down. But inside the burrows, the temperature varies only two to three degrees Centigrade. It's always around 8°–10° C. inside.

A steady temperature keeps the eggs from freezing or getting too hot. It helps the eggs hatch. In North America, only about half the eggs in open nests hatch. But over two thirds—a much greater number—of the eggs in hole nests, including burrows, hatch.

This kind of hatching success could be enough reason for a bird to nest underground. But there is even more reason for burrows after the eggs hatch. Now the burrows protect the young birds.

This is the case with the Kiwi. The hen-sized mother Kiwi lays one or two eggs in the burrow. Then she forgets about the whole affair. She has done her best for her young. Her eggs are large. There is much food, or yolk, inside the egg for the baby to grow on.

And the father Kiwi gives the chicks enough time to grow, too. He incubates the egg for seventy-five to eighty days, until it hatches. But he doesn't feed his newborn. Instead, the baby uses up the rest of the egg yolk while staying in the protection of the burrow.

Kiwi

Around six days pass. The baby Kiwi has used its food supply and is ready for something else to eat. One night, the father Kiwi leads it out of the burrow. Sometimes he even scratches on the ground, as if to say, "This is how you find food." And the little Kiwi finds its own worms and insects and fruit on the forest floor.

A baby Kiwi doesn't need a lot of help. Some Kiwi chicks even find their own way out of the burrow. But the sheltering burrow protects it until it can fend for itself.

Most of the other birds born in burrows need a great deal more help. Without the protection of burrows, they would be easy prey for enemies.

Consider the sea birds—the prions, storm-petrels, shearwaters, puffins, and penguins. Large gulls are a threat. The babies are protected by resting in places the gulls can't easily pillage. A burrow is a good answer to the threat of the marauding gulls.

The gulls are a threat even to the fully grown parent sea birds. They attack the parents, hoping to eat either them or the food they are bringing to the young. So puffins burrow as close to the edge of the land as they can get. They move in and out quickly and escape the gulls. Prions and storm-petrels and shearwaters also try to avoid the gulls. They do it by coming home late and leaving early. They travel in the dark when the squadrons of gulls are sleeping.

Burrows give protection, but they are dark. How can parent birds find their eggs and, later, their young so they can take care of them?

Most of the eggs of birds that nest aboveground have colors

and speckles and other markings. The markings help protect the eggs by hiding them—camouflaging them from enemies.

But at first, probably all birds' eggs were white. Eggs in an underground nest had no need for markings because they were hidden already. So the eggs of most burrowing birds are white. In the dark nest, white eggs are easier for the adult birds to find and incubate than colored, camouflaged eggs would be.

When the chicks hatch, they behave in ways that will make it easy for their parents to find them. Most newborn birds instinctively gape when the burrow grows completely dark for a moment. That darkness means that a food-bringer has blotted out even the tiny amount of light that comes in the entrance. And some gaping baby birds have reflector parts in their mouths which help guide their parents to them in the dark burrows.

Why does a bird go underground?

Because going underground works. The burrow is snug and the temperature inside is steady. The burrow gives protection.

A nest underground is what burrowing birds want. What is inside is a secret. And keeping it secret means surviving.

List of Scientific Names

Manx Shearwater	*Puffinus puffinus*
Short-tailed Shearwater	*Puffinus tenuirostris*
Common Shelduck	*Tadorna tadorna*
Snow Finches	*Montifringilla* sp.
Kakapo	*Strigops habroptilus*
Kiwi	*Apteryx australis*
Sand Martin or Bank Swallow	*Riparia riparia*
Crab Plover	*Dromas ardeola*
European Kingfisher	*Alcedo atthis*
Kookaburra	*Dacelo gigas*
Blue-crowned Motmot	*Momotus momota*
Todies	*Todidae*
Red-throated Bee-eater	*Merops bulocki*
White-fronted Nunbird	*Monasa morphoeus*
Fairy Prion	*Pachyptila turtur*
Burrowing Owl	*Athene cunicularia*
Little Penguin	*Eudyptula minor*
Common Puffin	*Fratercula arctica*
Wilson's Storm-Petrel	*Oceanites oceanicus*
African River Martin	*Pseudochelidon eurystomina*
White-eyed River Martin	*Pseudochelidon sirintarae*

Index

Italics indicate illustration